Conscious Bible Stories

Cain & Abel

J. Aedo

Conscious Bible Stories
Cain & Abel

Children's Books For Conscious Parents

© 2022, Jay Aedo

www.consciousbiblestories.com

Author:
Jay Aedo, www.consciousbiblestories.com

Cover Design, Illustration:
QBN Studios, www.qbnstudios.com

Editing, Proofreading:
Wiebke Tasch, Poolak Stags, Angela Nguyen

Publishing Consulting:
Digital Authors LLC, www.digital-authors.com

Website Design:
Adamo Vittiglio

ISBN: 979-8-9859003-0-9

The work, including its parts, is protected by copyright. Any exploitation is prohibited without the consent of the author. This applies in particular to electronic or other reproduction, translation, distribution and making available to the public.

Conscious Bible Stories is a series of children's books. In this edition; Cain and Abel, is based on the original characters of the Bible. Where Cain came to be known as the man who became so jealous and enraged that he killed his brother, Abel in cold blood.

The story has been repeated on a loop throughout the history of the world Imprinting mankind with a belief that we are the descendants of a man who killed his own brother.

Essentially, we have inherited the program that automatically reacts to feelings of anger, resentment and jealousy.

The timeline created by the original Bible story is antiquated. It's time for an update.

Conscious Bible Stories intends to share a different story as to where we come from. Redefining who we are, what we're made of, and where we're going as mankind on planet Earth. It points us toward a different direction. Implying a new narrative where we are no longer caught in the karmic momentum of the unconscious history. We have the conscious awareness now to create Ourstory.

The first born sons of Adam and Eve were named Cain and Abel.

Growing up, Cain often had a misunderstanding within himself. He couldn't figure out why his little brother, Abel, seemed to always get what he wanted out of life. Sometimes, this misunderstanding caused Cain to feel anger.

Cain struggled with this, so one day he finally asked, "how do you always get what you want, brother?"

"I make sacrifices for God," Abel responded.

"What's a sacrifice?" Cain asked curiously.

"A sacrifice is when you dream of something greater than yourself and then you do what it takes to make your dream a reality," Abel said excitedly.

"Hmm, I don't get it. Can you show me?"
Cain asked.

"Of course," said Abel. "What I do is this: I offer the best of what I have. As a shepherd I know my sheep very well and can tell which one is the best.

I pick that one and I offer it to God as a sacrifice. You can do that too. You're a good farmer, right? Go and pick out the best of your crops. Offer them to God and see what happens."

Cain went on to do what Abel told him. But when picking out his crops, he did not choose the best. He chose the older and uglier vegetables and offered that to God as his sacrifice.

Cain saw Abel the next day walking around with a new coat. "Where'd you get that new coat?" Cain demanded in frustration.

"God. Where else?" responded Abel, as if pointing out the obvious.

After that, Cain felt jealous, and a deeply-rooted anger arose within him. As a result he decided to trick his own brother into death.

Cain plotted to kill Abel.

Once they get deep in the fields, Cain starts acting erratically, and comes at Abel aggressively swinging a rock.

Abel saw it coming, by simply being disciplined and composed within Himself.

Abel dodged Cain's wild swings, grabbed him from behind and choked him unconscious.

While Cain regained consciousness, he felt dazed and confused. He looked up at Abel and wondered what happened.

Abel declared the truth. "You tried to kill me, and I stopped you. Why did you do that?"

Cain had no choice but to confess his truth. "God favored your sacrifice over mine and I became so jealous and angry that all I could think about was ending your life."

"What makes you think God favored my sacrifice over yours?" asked Abel. "I thought your gift was unique and wonderful."

"You thought that?" asked Cain in surprise.
"I thought it was old and ugly."

"Why would you think that?" Abel asked. "You were supposed to offer your best."

"I know, but at the very last minute, I changed my mind. I wanted to save the best for myself and our family," said Cain.

Abel saw the misunderstanding within Cain and asked, "don't you know who God is, my brother?"

"No, who is that? Why do you give your best to God? And why does God give you gifts?"

Abel then revealed: "When I say, I give my best to God, I mean I give the best of Myself for the benefit of Myself and everything around me.

My coat, that you admire so much, I made it with my best sheep for my own comfort and warmth. God is not separate from you, my brother.

You are everything God is and much more. God is that conscious awareness within Yourself. You're just a little confused.

Look at how you already gave your best to God, because you saved the best of what you had for Yourself and your family. Can you see that?"

Cain realized what Abel was showing him and immediately felt a deep sense of regret. He was ashamed and begged his brother for forgiveness.

But Abel had already forgiven him. Which is why He decided to fight for what He believed in. To talk things out with His brother, instead of seeking revenge.

Abel asked for Cain's forgiveness, for leading him to believe that God was separate from him.

Cain felt a deep sense of gratitude for the mercy and compassion his brother had shown. From that day on, He vowed to always give the best of what He had to God.

And as *Ourstory* goes, Cain and Abel cleared up all the misunderstandings between each other and within themselves. One day, they left home and went out into the unknown.

They met many people and built great cities together. Everywhere they went, they shared their story of triumph over the simple misunderstanding that almost caused a lifetime of confusion and suffering.

We are the ascendants of Our great ancestors, Cain and Abel. The brave brothers who live forever within Us.

CPSIA information can be obtained
at www.ICGtesting.com
Printed in the USA
JSHW041214180822
29387JS00002B/47